VILLAGE ECONOMICS
A STORYBOOK ON ECONOMIC THEORIES

Written by
Chris Anderson

Illustrated by
Daniel Ringenberg

Kendall Hunt
publishing company

Kendall Hunt
publishing company

www.kendallhunt.com
Send all inquiries to:
4050 Westmark Drive
Dubuque, IA 52004-1840

Copyright © 2022 by Kendall Hunt Publishing Company

PAK ISBN 979-8-7657-0561-2
Text Alone ISBN 979-8-7657-0562-9

Published in the United States of America

CONTENTS

INTRODUCTION

When I attended the University of Chicago's Graduate School of Business (now Chicago Booth), the campus looked about the same as it does today. Harper Library still looks like a castle. The cafeteria in the Reynolds Club building still looks the same. Students sit around the large wooden tables and talk about academic theories, and the walls are still lined with oil-painted portraits of past presidents of the university. I once sat at those tables too, after I left my engineering job at a local factory to pursue a formal business education.

My friends at the U of C had specific areas of study in mind. Paul, now at Fidelity, left his auditing position at KPMG to concentrate on Investment Theory. Pete left his position at Procter and Gamble to study Statistics, and Linda left her role at SBC to learn about Management Strategy. They were often sought out by our fellow students for their subject matter knowledge. I didn't get too many requests for academic guidance, but I was one of the locals there, and I was counted on for knowing the best places to get a pizza.

I was the only one at our lunch table at the U of C who brought in home-baked goods, and my friends were fascinated by the items my wife put in my brown bag lunches. They usually wanted to trade for them. While we were bartering, they would ask probing questions. What kind of bread is *that*? Are *those* things muffins? Why are they *orange*? I traded my home-baked items for store-bought items like Twinkies and Oreos. The voluntary exchanges at our lunch table were my first real lessons in Economics.

Milton Friedman had already gone to another university, but other big names in Economics were still there. Bud Fackler was my first Economics professor and my favorite. Before he taught at the U of C, he served as an economist for a past US President. Bud's unique way of teaching Economics through telling stories made the subject easy for me to understand.

I recently retired from a career in banking. For something fun to do, and because I have a passion for this subject, I teach undergraduate Economics at a college near my home. My students enjoy learning about economic theories, but they tend to have difficulty with the textbooks. To bring more clarity to their learning experiences, I use examples that everyone can relate to. I also tell my students stories that explain economic theories, like my favorite Economics professor did for me. Those experiences inspired me to write this storybook about Economics.

CHAPTER 1

GROSS DOMESTIC PRODUCT (GDP)

The value of a country's economic output.

GDP

There was once a shoemaker named Joseph who lived in a small village by the sea. He lived a simple but useful life, and the shoes he made were beautiful. Others in his village fished, baked bread, grew grapes, raised sheep, farmed, or made clothes. Everyone of working age earned money to buy the things they needed.

Joseph's village was known for its fine shoes and smoked fish. Other villages were known for things like the purest olive oil or the best wool. Buying, selling, and trading took place within each village and between villages. Items from Joseph's country were also transported to other countries and sold, and items from other countries were sent to his country to be bought.

Although this economic activity took place long ago, even before textbooks were written, Joseph's country produced the equivalent of what economists call *Gross Domestic Product (GDP)*. This statistic represents the monetary value of all the goods and services produced within a country's borders in an annual time period, plus the value of its net exports (exports minus imports).

You may have seen this equation in an Economics textbook.

$$GDP = C + G + I + NX$$

C is CONSUMER spending. Joseph used money earned from making shoes to buy bread for his family, and the baker used some of his earnings to buy a pair of Joseph's fine shoes.

G is GOVERNMENT spending. Joseph's government released funds to build roads and it paid government employees such as tax collectors.

I is capital INVESTMENT made by the public. For example, the baker bought bricks to build a new oven.

NX is NET EXPORTS, or the value of every item exported by Joseph's country minus the value of everything it imported.

Joseph thought about the shoes he made and how they contributed value to his family, his village, and his country. He also realized that the goods produced by everyone in his village and in his country could be totaled up to compute the size of their society. That is essentially what an Economy is—it is the size, or the value, of goods and services produced by a society. He may not have known what the term GDP was, but he did know that the shoes he made added value to the world he lived in.

Bringing his thoughts to terms and calculations economists would eventually use, Joseph estimated that the size of the economy in his country could be found by taking the quantity of everything produced, multiplying it by the price at which each item was sold, and adding up the total. This of course would have to be calculated every year for an accurate picture, because circumstances affecting the production of goods would change from year to year.

Today, if GDP for Joseph's small country was measured in US dollars, it would be around $2.6 trillion. This sum seems enormous, but it is small, compared to the United States, with its GDP of around $22.6 trillion.

CHAPTER 2

SCARCITY

People usually want more than they have.

SCARCITY

The shoes Joseph made were lovely and, at the same time, incredibly sturdy. His little shoe shop was not only visited by customers from his village but also from far away, because his shoes were awesome.

Unfortunately, certain circumstances limited the amount of shoes Joseph could produce. His wife and children depended on him for other things and there were only so many hours in a day. The sheep on the mountainside used for his leather were limited in quantity. He also had to choose between buying materials for his shoes or buying food and other essential items for his family. Just like you and me, Joseph lived in a world of *scarcity*. No one has unlimited resources, but almost everyone has unlimited wishes. In other words, he was ruled by his *budget,* and he faced *trade-offs.*

He had to follow his budget, and in a typical week he only had a certain amount of money to buy sheepskins for shoe leather and loaves of bread for his family. Any combination of these items he picked had to fall within his budget. Economists call these kinds of limitations *budget constraints.*

Imagine for a moment that Joseph's currency was in US dollars and his weekly budget for bread and sheepskins was $20. If a loaf of bread was $1, and a sheepskin was $4, he could only purchase certain combinations of those goods because any combination he chose could not exceed $20. At opposite extremes, he could purchase five sheepskins and no loaves of bread, or twenty loaves of bread and no sheepskins. He would most likely have chosen to buy four loaves of bread and four sheepskins, or eight loaves of bread and three sheepskins.

The following budget constraint model and budget table illustrate the possible combinations of sheepskins and bread that Joseph would be able to choose with his weekly budget of $20.

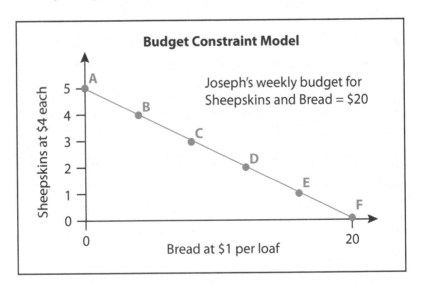

Point	Sheepskins	Bread	Total $ Cost
A	5	0	20 + 0 = 20
B	4	4	16 + 4 = 0
C	3	8	12 + 8 = 20
D	2	12	8 + 12 = 20
E	1	16	4 + 16 = 20
F	0	20	0 ı 20 = 20

As he thought about the trade-offs he needed to make to stay within his budget, Joseph realized there were costs to choosing one good over another. Something had to be given up to obtain something else. Economists call these kinds of trade-offs *opportunity costs*.

You may have seen these equations in an Economics textbook:

Budget = *Price s* × *Quantity s* + *Price b* × *Quantity b* = $20

Opportunity Cost for 1 sheepskin = *price s / price b*
    = *4 / 1, or 4 loaves of bread.*

Opportunity Cost for 1 loaf of bread = *price b / price s*
    = *1 / 4, or a quarter of a sheepskin.*

In other words, if Joseph chose to buy a sheepskin, that would prevent him from buying four loaves of bread. If he chose to buy a loaf of bread, he would have to give up the opportunity of buying a quarter of a sheepskin.

CHAPTER 3

TRADE

You cannot always *make* what you want.

TRADE

We know that Joseph's life was influenced by the theory of *Scarcity*, and that he was essentially ruled by his budget, like you and me and everyone else.

His ability to make gorgeous shoes brought in money, which allowed him to purchase the other goods and services his family needed. To describe the talent Joseph used to perform his job as a shoemaker, economists refer to the concept of *specialization*.

Imagine now that each person in Joseph's village was part of an overall process that produced dozens of goods and services. *Specialization* allowed workers to focus on the part of the production process where they had a distinct advantage. People in the village had different skills, talents, and interests, so they were better at some jobs than others. Joseph excelled at making shoes. Others in the village excelled at making bread, fishing nets, and clothes.

Specialization requires *trade*. Why? The people in Joseph's village had unique skills and talents. They earned money by employing their skills to produce what they were good at making, and they needed to buy things they did not produce.

Joseph's village traded with other villages, and his country traded with other countries. If we focus on trading activity between Joseph's country and other countries, how do we calculate the value of the trading activity? I have circled the last portion of the GDP equation you saw in the first chapter:

$$GDP = C + G + I + \boxed{NX}$$

The value of a country's *Net Exports* is represented by the *NX* portion of the equation.

You may remember from the first chapter that *net exports* equals the value of every item exported by Joseph's country minus the value of everything they imported.

Net Exports is represented by the equation below:

$$NX = exports - imports$$

Another equation you may have seen in Economics textbooks is the *exports to GDP* ratio. It is a generally accepted measure of a country's trading activity as a percentage of its total economic production:

$$exports / GDP$$

The components in the *exports to GDP* ratio are also found in the equation that computes GDP:

$$\boxed{GDP} = C + G + I + \boxed{exports} - imports$$

Joseph's country was a small country at the time of this story. Today, his country is still much smaller than the United States. It is a fact that small countries have larger *exports to GDP* ratios than big countries. Why? Small countries trade for *more* of what they need, because they produce *less* of what they need within their own borders than big countries produce. This fact is demonstrated below, using current statistics from Joseph's country and the United States.

Amounts are shown in trillions of US dollars:

Joseph's country today:

exports / GDP = .538 trillion / 2.611 trillion = 20.6%

The United States today:

exports / GDP = 1.644 trillion / 22.675 trillion = 7.3%

You cannot always *make* what you want. The statistics on this page show you that even though the economy in Joseph's country today is much smaller than the United States, his country's trade volume as a percentage of GDP is much larger.

CHAPTER 4

SUPPLY and DEMAND

Understanding production and consumption.

SUPPLY and DEMAND

Because Joseph's life was influenced by the theory of *Scarcity,* his budget limited his choices. He used a simple rule when he *purchased* items for his shoe shop and his family. If the price of an item went up, the quantity he purchased went down. If the price went down, the quantity he purchased went up. This rule is what economists call *The Law of Demand.* In other words, price moves in an *opposite direction* to the quantity demanded. Why? Because of the theory of *Scarcity.* People are essentially ruled by their budgets.

You may have seen these illustrations in an Economics textbook.

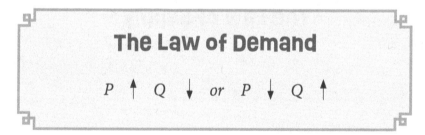

The Law of Demand

$$P \uparrow \quad Q \downarrow \quad or \quad P \downarrow \quad Q \uparrow$$

You have also learned so far that people cannot make everything they need to eat or use in their daily lives. They need to buy things that someone else produces.

Joseph lived in the southern portion of his country, where the terrain was hilly, and the soil was rocky. It was fine for growing olive trees and raising sheep, but not for cultivating wheat. His village had to buy wheat from the northern part of his country where it grew plentifully in a fertile river valley. That area supplied all the wheat consumed by Joseph's country, and much of the wheat used by surrounding countries.

Farmers in the northern part of Joseph's country followed a simple rule for *supplying* their agricultural products to customers. If the price they would receive for the products they supplied was going up, they increased the quantity they supplied, and if prices were going down, they decreased the quantity they supplied. This rule is what economists call *The Law of Supply*. In other words, price moves in the *same direction* as the quantity supplied.

You may have seen these illustrations in an Economics textbook.

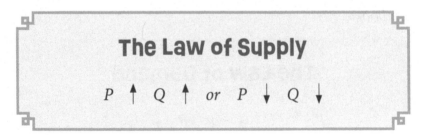

The Law of Supply

$$P \uparrow \ Q \uparrow \ \textit{or} \ P \downarrow \ Q \downarrow$$

I will go back to the *Law of Demand.* If it were to be shown in a diagram, it would look like the next diagram. Price is on the vertical axis and Quantity (demanded) is on the horizontal axis. The *Demand Line* in the diagram always runs diagonally from the upper left down to the lower right. If the price of wheat moves up, the diagram illustrates that the quantity demanded goes down. If the price of wheat goes down, the quantity demanded goes up. Why? Remember that people are essentially ruled by their budgets.

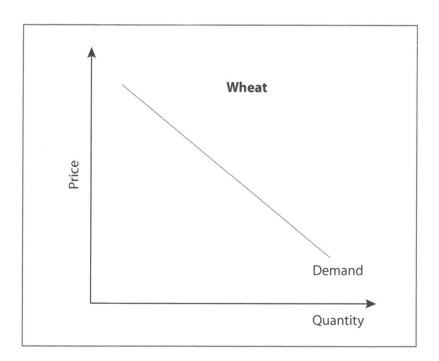

The *Law of Supply* is shown on the following diagram. Price is on the vertical axis and Quantity (supplied) is on the horizontal axis. The *Supply Line* always runs diagonally from the lower left up to the upper right. If the selling price for wheat moves up, the diagram illustrates that the quantity supplied goes up. If the selling price for wheat goes down, the quantity supplied goes down. Why? Suppliers want to maximize revenue and profits.

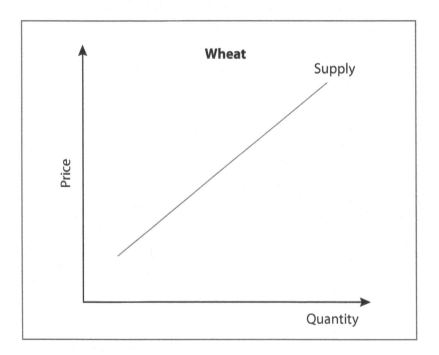

Demand and Supply Lines are both shown on the next diagram. Suppose the *market price* for wheat in Joseph's country was $4 US for each bushel supplied. At that price, farmers were willing to supply and consumers were willing to buy 3,000 bushels of wheat. This "point of agreement" on the diagram is what economists refer to as *a market in equilibrium.*

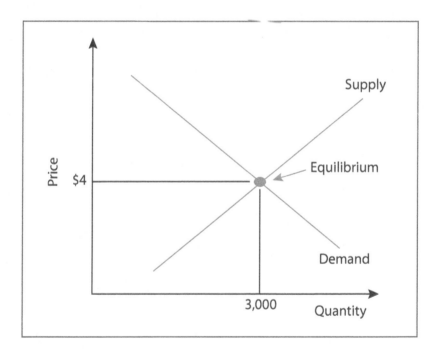

Now suppose that wheat prices occasionally changed in Joseph's country. A reason for the price of wheat *going down* was due to competitors entering the wheat market. When more farmers entered the market, this increased the amount of wheat produced, and it moved the Supply Line *to the right*. This caused the quantity available for sale to increase and prices to go down. Eventually, price and supply would have gone back to an equilibrium as weaker, less profitable competitors went out of business.

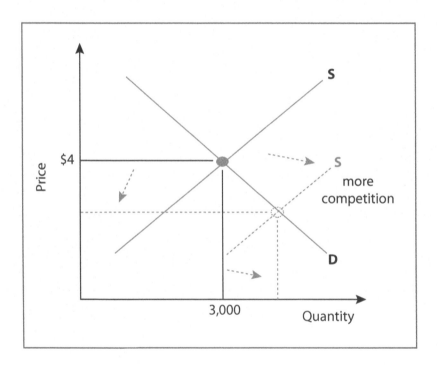

Prices also could have *increased* when there was a severely dry growing season. The Supply Line would have shifted to the left, reflecting a *lower supply* of wheat and a higher price per bushel. At the higher price, the quantity demanded would have decreased. Price and supply would have returned to a market equilibrium price of $4 and a quantity of 3,000 bushels after a more normal growing season.

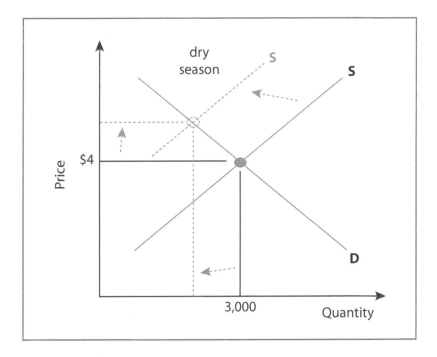

As Joseph learned about Supply and Demand theory, he gained a better understanding of how the world around him functioned on a day-to-day basis.

CHAPTER 5

ELASTICITY of DEMAND

How much people care or don't care
when prices change.

ELASTICITY of DEMAND

Joseph learned that *Demand* was influenced by the theory of Scarcity. In other words, he was aware that he had a budget and that influenced what items and how much he could buy with his budget. He also thought about how sensitive he was to price changes, and he realized he was extremely sensitive to price changes on certain items, but not as sensitive to price changes on other items. Economists refer to this perceived sensitivity to price changes as the *Elasticity of Demand*, and they have established a formula to calculate this sensitivity as an *Elasticity Value*.

You may have seen this equation in an Economics textbook.

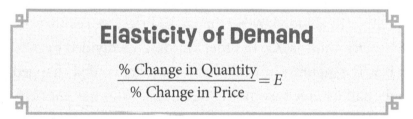

Elasticity of Demand

$$\frac{\% \text{ Change in Quantity}}{\% \text{ Change in Price}} = E$$

Elasticity of Demand is also referred to as Price Elasticity of Demand. More Demand Lines will be demonstrated to show that different products have different Elasticity of Demand values.

Example 1: Wine (Inelastic)

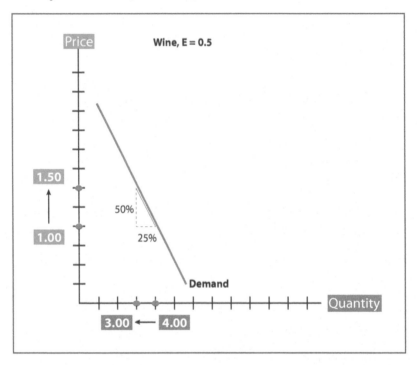

Notice that the Demand Line for wine is shown as a steep angle. If wine went up in *price* by 50%, the *quantity* Joseph bought, or demanded, would go down by only 25%.

Using the equation for Elasticity of Demand, % Change in Quantity divided by % Change in Price, we see that the *Elasticity Value* is *0.5*. In other words, 25% divided by 50% = 0.5. The *quantity* of wine that Joseph demanded changed only half as much as the change in *price*, so the *Elasticity Value* is *E = 0.5*.

Even today, wine has an Elasticity Value of around 0.5, and since it is less than 1, economists refer to wine as being *inelastic* as it relates to demand. Wine is not on sale as much as the other products consumers buy. In fact, the opposite is true. Stores can make more money by raising the price of wine. For every 1% increase in price, the demand for wine will go down by only 0.5%, because E = 0.5.

Joseph enjoyed drinking wine and his *sensitivity* to price changes on wine was *low*.

Example 2: Restaurant Meals (Elastic)

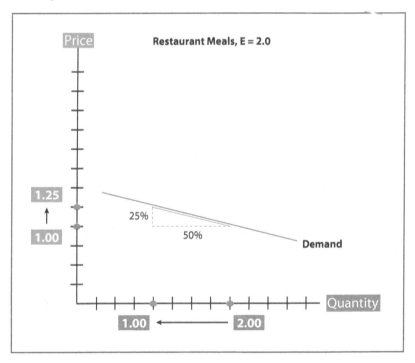

Notice that the Demand Line for a restaurant meal is shown at a shallow angle. Joseph liked to take his wife and children out for a meal at the restaurants in his village, but he was *very sensitive* to price changes on those meals. If the *price* for a restaurant meal went *up* by 25%, the *quantity* he purchased, or demanded, went *down* by 50%, which was twice the percentage change in price.

Using the equation for Elasticity of Demand, % Change in Quantity divided by % Change in Price, we see that the *Elasticity Value, or E,* for a restaurant meal is 2.0. In other words, 50% divided by 25% = 2.0. Joseph's *sensitivity* to price changes in restaurant meals was *very high* because $E = 2.0$ for restaurant meals.

When restaurant meals occasionally went on sale, or *down* in price, the opposite was true. Joseph's demand for those meals went *up* by twice the percentage change of the price decrease.

Most restaurant meals today have an elasticity value of around 2.0, and since that value is more than 1, economists refer to a restaurant meal as being *elastic* as it relates to demand. You may have guessed that restaurants frequently have price reduction specials on their meals. Why wouldn't they? For every 1% reduction in price, the demand for their meals will go up by 2%, because $E = 2.0$.

Joseph cared much more when restaurant meal prices changed than he did when there was a change in the price of his favorite bottle of wine. Why? You have learned that restaurant meals are *elastic*, with an *Elasticity Value* of 2.0, and wine is *inelastic*, with an *Elasticity Value* of 0.5.

CHAPTER 6

MARKET STRUCTURES and PRODUCTION COSTS

A simpler explanation.

MARKET STRUCTURES and PRODUCTION COSTS

The marketplace in the center of Joseph's village teemed with merchants and customers on Saturdays and Sundays. All kinds of things were bought and sold there. Joseph closed his shoe shop and went down to the marketplace with his family to sell his shoes on the first weekend of every month. He also shopped for other items and visited with the people he knew. It was always fascinating for him to see the variety of items for sale.

Many items were identical and priced the same, no matter how many merchants sold them. Economists refer to this type of market structure as *Perfect Competition*.

Some items for sale were only sold by one merchant. They could not be found anywhere else in the village, and they were the highest priced items in the marketplace. Economists refer to this kind of market structure as a *Monopoly*.

Other items were sold by several merchants. These items were similar, but not the same, and the merchants priced them differently. For example, Joseph could sell his shoes for a higher price than the shoes made by other shoemakers in the marketplace. Economists call this type of market structure *Imperfect Competition*.

We will take a closer look at these market structures in this chapter.

Perfect Competition

Joseph's cousin, Antonio, was one of the many merchants who sold ground wheat at the marketplace in his village. Customers were willing to pay $1 per pound for the ground wheat. Antonio and his competitors were willing to sell the ground wheat for $1 per pound. On a typical weekend, 1,000 pounds of ground wheat was sold at the marketplace. Demand and Supply lines crossed at the intersection where the price was $1, and 1,000 pounds of ground wheat was supplied. In other words, the intersection of the lines was located where Supply equaled Demand.

If Antonio raised his price for ground wheat to $1.10 per pound, *even his own sister would not buy it* from him. She could get the same product from another merchant for $1 per pound. Ground wheat was a perfectly competitive product in Joseph's village.

Price *and* revenue from the sale of each unit of ground wheat were the same *at any quantity* in Perfect Competition. Therefore, *marginal revenue* in this market structure was represented by a *horizontal line*. The next diagram illustrates this relationship between price and marginal revenue.

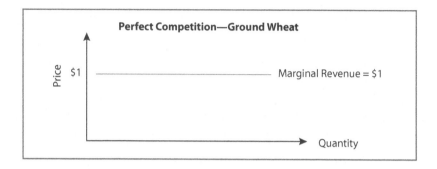

When he saw Antonio selling ground wheat, Joseph asked him an important question. If Antonio couldn't change his price for ground wheat, what could he do to maximize his profits?

Antonio's production costs are shown in the next diagram. In this market structure, *he could not control his price*, but he could produce to a quantity that would maximize his profits. He produced 90 pounds of ground wheat, where his *marginal cost equaled his marginal revenue*.

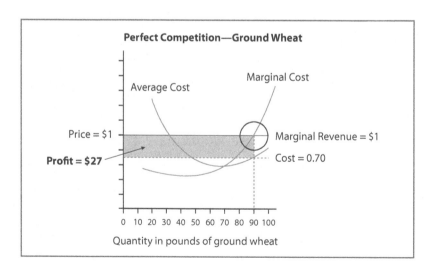

Marginal costs are costs associated with producing each additional unit of production. Antonio stopped producing and selling at 90 pounds, because he would have to employ more workers and tools if he produced more than 90 pounds of ground wheat, and each pound he produced after that amount would cost more than the selling price of $1. So, his answer to Joseph's question was, he could control his quantity to maximize profit.

Total revenue at 90 pounds was $90, or 90 × $1, and total cost was $63, or 90 × $0.70. His profit was ($1 − $0.70) × 90 = $27.

You may have seen these equations in an Economics textbook:

Total Revenue = quantity sold × selling price
Profit = Total Revenue − Total Cost
Total Cost = *Fixed* plus *Variable* costs
Fixed Costs = *expenses that stay the same*
Variable Costs = *expenses that change as quantities change*
Average Cost = *Avg. Fixed Cost* + *Avg. Variable Cost*

Fixed costs in this case would have been the cost of Antonio's rent for his workshop. *Variable costs* would have been any expense that varied as production quantities changed, such as wages he paid to employees or the amount of raw wheat he purchased to produce the ground wheat.

It was stated previously that *Marginal Revenue* will always be the same value at any quantity in Perfect Competition. In this example, it was $1. Antonio would get $1 for each pound of ground wheat he produced and sold.

Here is the equation for Marginal Revenue:

$$\text{Marginal Revenue} = \frac{\text{Change in Total Revenue}}{\text{Change in Quantity}}$$

It was also stated previously that Marginal Costs will vary with production. Those costs apply to each additional unit produced. As more pounds of ground wheat were produced and sold, Marginal Costs would have increased. Here is the equation for Marginal Cost:

$$\text{Marginal Cost} = \frac{\text{Change in Total Cost}}{\text{Change in Quantity}}$$

The revenue, cost, and profit concepts covered so far in this chapter are key elements of what economists refer to as *Theories of the Firm*.

Monopoly

Now we should look at the *opposite* of a perfectly competitive market structure in Joseph's village marketplace. Rather than being in a market where merchants must price to the *market price*, a *monopoly* is a market structure with *no competition* at all, and a *monopolist* has complete market power and control over prices.

Mario the gemstone merchant was a *monopolist*. For centuries, his family controlled the acquisition and sale of fine gemstones. He was originally from a country to the south, across the sea, and his family owned the land where the gemstones were mined. He sold his gemstones in Joseph's village, and his siblings and cousins sold their gemstones in other villages across the region. Since Mario faced no competition, *he could charge any price he wished.*

Monopolists create barriers that prevent competitors from entering their markets. In this example, Mario and his family controlled a physical resource: gemstones.

In the perfectly competitive market structure you saw earlier, *marginal revenue* was a *horizontal line* extending *left to right*, from the price axis. The market set the price, and it remained the same at every quantity produced and sold. In contrast, the next diagram represents a *monopolistic market structure*. The marginal revenue line for a monopolist is *not* a horizontal line. It extends from the upper left to the lower right, and it is positioned to the left of the Demand Line. The monopolist sets the price in this market structure, and price affects revenue.

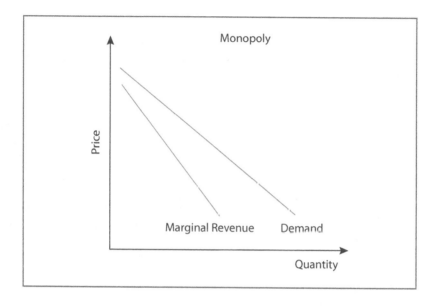

Why does the marginal revenue line have a different shape in a monopolistic market structure than it did in a perfectly competitive market structure? Remember *Scarcity* and the *Law of Demand*? Mario the monopolist could set *high prices* for his gemstones because he had no competition, but his customers would still have been *price sensitive*. If he lowered his prices, he could have sold more gemstones, but his *marginal revenue* and *profit* would have gone down.

You are correct if you guessed that Mario would not have wanted to lower his prices.

You can see in the next diagram that Mario stopped selling gemstones at the point where *marginal cost = marginal revenue*. Why? Past that point, marginal cost was higher than marginal revenue.

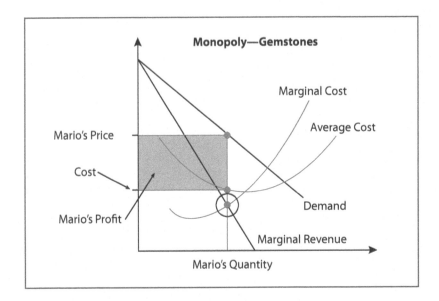

Mario's price, costs, and quantity shown in the next diagram further illustrate where he maximized his profit. He produced and sold 10 gemstones every weekend at the marketplace.

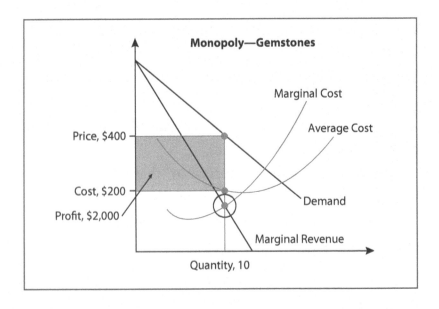

His profit was (Price – Cost) × Quantity, or ($400 – $200) × 10 = $2,000. That's not bad for a typical weekend at the marketplace!

What would have happened if Mario lowered his prices to sell more gemstones? In the next diagram (notice the dotted lines on the diagram), 14 customers would have agreed to buy gemstones for $300 each. His profit would have been $1,400, or ($300 – $200) × 14 = $1,400. Lowering his prices would have *added* 1 more customers, but it would have also *lowered* his profits by $600. No self-respecting monopolist would do that. Why not? Because they have *no* competitors, monopolists will always want to maximize profits.

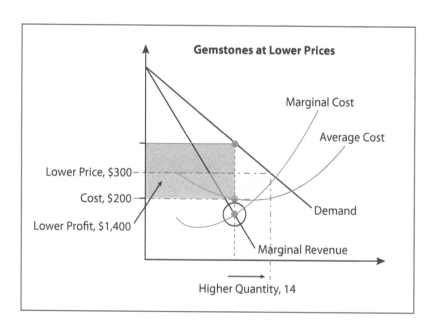

Imperfect Competition

As you can imagine, Joseph's shoe stall at the marketplace in his village was always crowded with customers. They adored his shoes. The leather on the outside of his shoes was soft and supple, but the leather on the inside of them was like a dream. While he fitted and sold his shoes, his family watched closely over the remaining shoes, so they would not be stolen. Joseph's family name was proudly stamped on the inside of each shoe (that same name can still be found today on his family's shoes, and they sell for $900 or more per pair).

Joseph sold his shoes within a market structure that economists refer to as *Imperfect Competition, or Monopolistic Competition*. It is positioned between Perfect Competition and Monopoly, and many consumer products today are sold in this market structure. Luxury cars and designer clothing are good examples.

Joseph differentiated his shoes from those of other shoemakers in a few ways: physical aspects of his product, a money-back guarantee, and perceptions about his product, true or not. Products that are distinctive in one or more of these areas are what economists call *differentiated products*.

When a producer like Joseph could differentiate his products, he could charge higher prices and maximize his profits. Joseph's prices and costs are shown below.

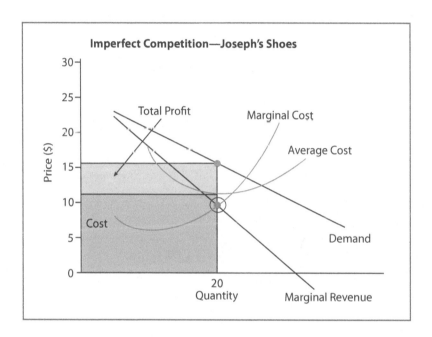

We can see also that Joseph chose to stop production where *marginal cost = marginal revenue* at 20 pairs of shoes. He maximized profit at that point. He would lose money on shoes produced and sold after 20 pairs, because after that point marginal costs would exceed marginal revenue.

We saw that the shape of the *marginal revenue* line on the diagram was downward sloping. Why? Joseph's shoes were highly sought after, but due to the theory of *Scarcity*, customers were still price sensitive.

The next diagram shows that Joseph priced his shoes at $15.50 per pair and his cost was $10.50 per pair. His profit was $100, or (Price – Cost) × Quantity. Differently stated, profit is shown as ($15.50 – $10.50) × 20 = $100.

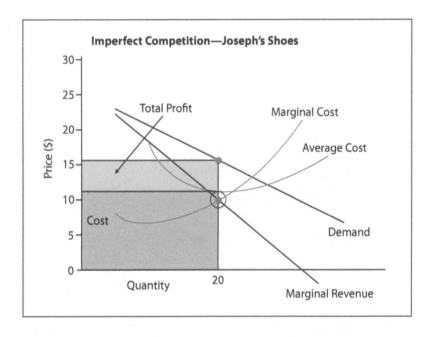

Joseph and Mario's market structures both faced downward sloping Demand and Marginal Revenue lines, but unlike Mario, who had *no* competition, Joseph needed to compete in his market structure.

New competitors occasionally entered the shoe market, and that *decreased* demand for Joseph's shoes. When that happened, he had to lower his prices and he sold less pairs of shoes. He either broke even or he made a smaller profit. Weaker competitors eventually went out of business, and

Joseph's prices returned to $15.50 per pair when they left the shoe market.

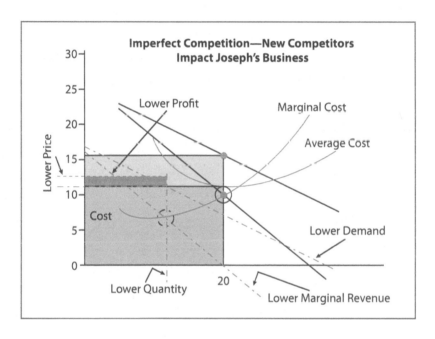

Demand and Marginal Revenue lines for Joseph's shoes shifted left (see the dotted lines on the previous diagram) when he faced increased competition and the Demand and Marginal Revenue lines stayed to the left until weaker competitors exited the market.

As this story has progressed, you have seen key concepts on *Scarcity, Supply and Demand, Market Structures,* and *Theories of the Firm* at work in Joseph's village. You may have noticed that economic theories build upon each other, and they work together to help explain how the world works on a day-to-day basis.

Consumption and production theories like the *Law of Demand* and the *Law of Supply* impacted buying and selling decisions in the three market structures you learned about.

In the next (and last) chapter of this book, we will focus on *Consumer Choice Theory*. How *do* people make purchasing decisions? You will find that out as we meet Joseph's wife, Sophia, and we see how she analyzes her shopping decisions.

CHAPTER 7

CONSUMER CHOICES

How *do* people make decisions?

CONSUMER CHOICES

Everyone in Joseph's village had their own individual tastes and preferences. If preferences alone drove decisions, they would have gotten *everything* they wished for. An individual's income and *another factor* weigh heavily in the human decision-making process. This additional factor is *satisfaction*. You will learn that people make decisions based on the *satisfaction they receive* from their choices. Economists refer to this type of satisfaction as *utility* and they use the concept of *utility values* to measure *consumer satisfaction*.

Scarcity was introduced in the second chapter of this book. You saw that Joseph made choices in consumption decisions based on what he could afford. He followed his weekly budget to purchase sheepskins and bread. That was your first example of a *budget constraint model*. He chose combinations of sheepskins and loaves of bread that would meet his needs. He also had to stay within his *budget*.

Joseph's wife, Sophia, purchased things for her family too. She wanted Joseph and their two children to look nice, so keeping her family's clothing up to date was important to her. Sophia was also crazy about culture, and she wanted her family to attend as many Plays as possible each month.

Just like Joseph, she needed to stay within her budget as she purchased those items.

The next diagrams illustrate Sophia's *budget constraint model,* with Plays on the vertical axis and Togas on the horizontal axis. One play cost $7 for the family to attend, and one shopping trip to buy a toga for each family member cost $14.

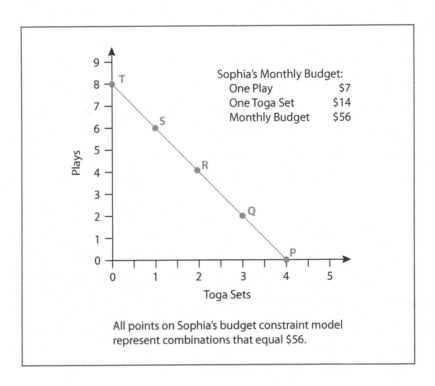

Sophia's Monthly Budget:
One Play $7
One Toga Set $14
Monthly Budget $56

All points on Sophia's budget constraint model represent combinations that equal $56.

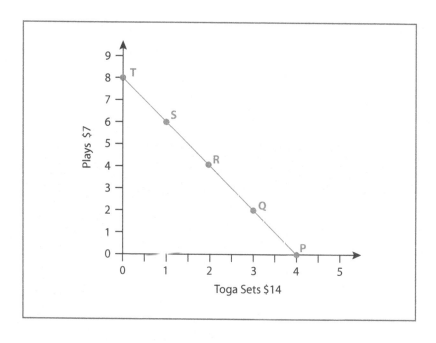

Legend for the points on the previous diagrams:

T = 8 family trips to Plays and 0 Togas, or 8 × $7 = $56

S = 6 Plays and 1 Toga for each member of the family, or (6 × $7) + (1 × $14) = $56

R = 4 Plays and 2 Togas for each member of the family, or (4 × $7) + (2 × $14) = $56

Q = 2 Plays and 3 Togas for each member of the family, or (2 × $7) + (3 × $14) = $56

P = 4 Togas for each member of the family and zero Plays, or 4 × $14 = $56

The tables shown on the following pages represent the satisfaction, or *utility*, that Sophia receives from purchasing

Plays and Toga sets for her family. Total utility is shown as a *cumulative value* at each quantity, and it *increases* as quantities increase. Marginal utility *decreases* every time an additional quantity is purchased.

Quantity Plays	Total Utility	Marginal Utility
1	16	16
2	31	15
3	45	14
4	58	13
5	70	12
6	81	11
7	91	10
8	100	9

Quantity Toga Sets	Total Utility	Marginal Utility
1	22	22
2	43	21
3	63	20
4	81	18
5	97	16
6	111	14
7	123	12
8	133	10

These statistics are now shown side by side.

Quantity Plays	Total Utility	Marginal Utility	Quantity Toga Sets	Total Utility	Marginal Utility
1	(16)	16	1	22	22
2	31	15	2	43	21
3	45	14	3	63	20
4	58	13	4	81	18
5	70	12	5	97	16
6	81	11	6	111	14
7	91	(10)	7	123	12
8	(100)	9	8	133	10

A *Total Utility value* represents the satisfaction or utility Sophia receives from a *cumulative quantity* of Plays or Togas. For example, it was only 16 when she purchased the first Play, and it was 100 for 8 Plays.

Marginal Utility, or *MU*, is the satisfaction, or utility, received from each *additional* purchase, and it goes down as more items are purchased.

You may have seen this equation in an Economics textbook:

$$MU = \frac{\text{Change in Total Utility}}{\text{Change in Quantity}}$$

For example, *Marginal Utility* was only 10 for the seventh Play Sophia purchased, or $(91 - 81) / (7 - 6) = 10$. For the eighth Play, it was only 9.

Why are *Marginal Utility* values *decreasing* as the number of items purchased increases in the table you saw on the previous page? When you buy your favorite drink or sandwich, and you keep on consuming those items in succession, the first items taste better than the last ones, don't they? This feeling you get and the *utility value statistics* you have seen demonstrate the *Law of Diminishing Marginal Utility*. It is an important law that helps explain *Consumer Choice Theory*.

How could Sophia have used her perceived utility values to arrive at an optimal purchasing decision? Remember the budget constraint model for her Play and Toga purchases? There were five possible combinations she could choose, and all of them met her monthly budget of $56. Which point on the next diagram *should* she have picked?

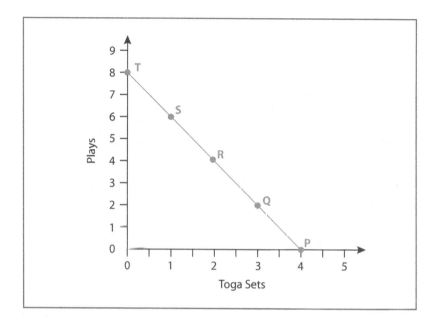

Economists believe that people will normally pick a combination of goods that gives them their *highest total utility value*. They believe she would have picked point S.

Sophia's total utility values are shown in the following diagrams. How and why she may have chosen a particular combination of Plays and Togas will be illustrated and explained.

Method #1

*Determining a Combination with
the Highest Total Utility*

Quantity Plays	Total Utility Plays	Marginal Utility Plays	Quantity Togas	Total Utility Togas	Marginal Utility Togas
1	16	16	1	(22)	22
2	31	15	2	43	21
3	45	14	3	63	20
4	58	13	4	81	18
5	70	12	5	97	16
6	(81)	11	6	111	14
7	91	10	7	123	12
8	100	9	8	133	10

Point	Plays	Togas	Combined Total Utility
P	0	4	$0 + 81 = 81$
Q	2	3	$31 + 63 = 94$
R	4	2	$58 + 43 = 101$
(S)	(6)	(1)	$81 + 22 = (103)$
T	8	0	$100 + 0 = 100$

The combination of items with the highest total utility is represented on the next diagram by point S: 6 Plays and 1 set of Togas.

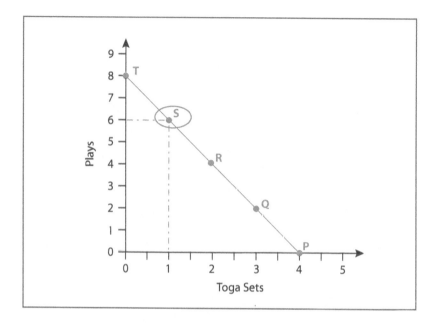

Sophia chose the combination of goods that provided her with the *highest total utility* value (103): 6 Plays and 1 set of Togas.

An additional method used in *Consumer Choice Theory* shows us that people care a lot about *the level of satisfaction per dollar* they spend. They measure *utility and satisfaction* when they purchase combinations of items by determining the *Marginal Utility divided by the Price* of the items they are choosing.

You may have seen these equations in an Economics textbook:

$$\text{Marginal Utility Per Dollar} = \frac{\text{Marginal Utility}}{\text{Price}}$$

$$\frac{MU_1}{Price_1} = \frac{MU_2}{Price_2}$$

The second equation above shows you that a consumer will find an optimal combination of items to purchase, where the marginal utility divided by price is the *same number* for each product in their purchasing decision.

The combination that Sophia picked using this *second* decision method is shown in the following table.

Method #2

Finding where MU/price is the same for each product. Remember that Plays cost $7 and Togas cost $14

Quantity of Plays	Total Utility	Marginal Utility	Marginal Utility per Dollar	Quantity Toga Sets	Total Utility	Marginal Utility	Marginal Utility per Dollar
1	16	16	16/$7 = 2.3	(1)	22	22	22/$14 = (1.6)
2	31	15	15/$7 = 2.14	2	43	21	21/$14 = 1.5
3	45	14	14/$7 = 2	3	63	20	20/$14 = 1.4
4	58	13	13/$7 = 1.9	4	81	18	18/$14 = 1.3
5	70	12	12/$7 = 1.7	5	97	16	16/$14 = 1.1
(6)	81	11	11/$7 = (1.6)	6	111	14	14/$14 = 1
7	91	10	10/$7 = 1.4	7	123	12	12/$14 = 1.2

6 Plays and 1 set of Togas optimizes Marginal Utility per dollar:

$$\frac{MU\ \text{play}}{Price\ \text{play}} = 1.6 \quad \text{and} \quad \frac{MU\ \text{toga}}{Price\ \text{toga}} = 1.6$$

Optimizing consumer purchase utility through finding the combination of goods with the highest total utility value, *or* through finding the combination of goods where each item in the purchasing decision has the *same* Marginal Utility per dollar, would have given Sophia the *same* answer: 6 Plays and 1 set of Togas.

That's the end of this book . . .

Joseph, his wife Sophia, and others in his village experienced the impact of economic theories in their daily lives. Economics is all around you. If you look for them, you'll be able to recognize economic theories at work in your world.

REFERENCES

Concepts and theories demonstrated in this book can be found in:

OpenStax, Principles of Microeconomics. OpenStax. © 2017 Rice University. https://d3bxy9euw4e147.cloudfront.net/ oscms-prodcms/media/documents/ PrinciplesofMicroeconomics-LR.pdf. Rice University, Houston, TX.

Statistics on Trade can be found in:

wits.worldbank.org., World Integrated Trade Solution.

Statistics on GDP can be found in:

https://www.worldometers.info/gdp/gdp-by-country/.

```
┌─────────────────────────────┐
│        QUESTIONS            │
│      and SOLUTIONS          │
└─────────────────────────────┘
```

Chapter 1

Gross Domestic Product (GDP)

1. Identify the correct equation below for Gross Domestic Product (GDP).

   a. $GDP = G + C - I + NX$
   b. $GDP = C + G + I - NX$
   c. $GDP = C + G + I + NX$
   d. $GDP = G - C - I + NX$

   For the questions shown below, fill in the correct symbols (letters a through d) in the blank spaces by the components in the GDP equation (numbers).

2. Consumer Spending   ____   a. NX
3. Capital Investments   ____   b. G
4. Net Exports   ____   c. I
5. Government Spending   ____   d. C

6. GDP is normally calculated for a country when?

    a. Daily
    b. Yearly
    c. Monthly
    d. Bi-annually

7. GDP measures what, for a country?

    a. Trade volume
    b. Rainfall in inches
    c. Economic production
    d. Population

8. Joseph imagined a rough calculation that would determine the size of his country's economy (i.e., GDP). What was it?

    a. Counting the number of all items sold in a year
    b. Counting the number of all items sold in a decade
    c. Taking the quantity of everything produced in a year, multiplying it by the price at which each item was sold, and adding up the total
    d. Taking the quantity of everything produced in a year, multiplying it by the cost at which each item was produced, and adding up the total

9. What is the definition of an Economy, as it was described in Chapter 1?

   a. It is the value of goods and services produced by a society each year
   b. It is the population of the country multiplied by the average price of the goods they produce
   c. It is the population of the country multiplied by the average cost of the goods they produce
   d. None of the above answers are correct

Chapter 2
Scarcity

1. No one has unlimited resources, but almost everyone has unlimited wishes. This sentence describes a concept in Economics known as:

    a. Austerity
    b. Prosperity
    c. Poverty
    d. Scarcity

2. Just like you and me, Joseph experienced the concept of Scarcity. Because of this, he was ruled by his:

    a. Family
    b. Budget
    c. Appetite
    d. Village

3. Joseph only had a certain amount of money to buy sheepskins for shoe leather and loaves of bread for his family. Because of this, he faced:

    a. Poverty
    b. Diversity
    c. Trade-offs
    d. Dilemmas

4. People buy combinations of items that fall within their budgets. Whatever combination they choose, the total cost of the items must fall within their budgets. A simple economic model used to demonstrate this concept is called a:

   a. Budget framework
   b. Spending model
   c. Quandary
   d. Budget constraint

5. Joseph realized there were costs to choosing one good over another. Something had to be given up to obtain something else. These kinds of costs are called:

   a. Fixed costs
   b. Variable costs
   c. Opportunity costs
   d. Sunk costs

6. Price s × Quantity s + Price b × Quantity b describes a budget equation when Joseph is buying sheepskins (s) and bread (b). What is the correct equation for the opportunity cost of 1 sheepskin?

   a. price s / price b
   b. price b / price s
   c. price b – price s
   d. price b + price s

7. Joseph's budget constraint model for sheepskins and bread is shown below. What observations can be drawn from the diagram?

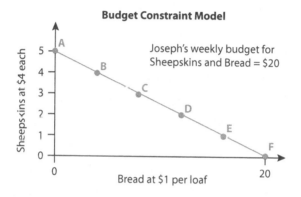

Budget Constraint Model

Joseph's weekly budget for
Sheepskins and Bread = $20

Sheepskins at $4 each

Bread at $1 per loaf

a. Any point shown on the diagonal line in the diagram will equal $20

b. Any point above the diagonal line in the diagram would equal a value > $20

c. Any point below the diagonal line in the diagram would equal a value < $20

d. All of the answers listed are correct

Chapter 3
Trade

1. To describe the talent Joseph used to perform his job as a shoemaker, economists refer to the concept of:

    a. Raw talent
    b. Specialization
    c. Diligence
    d. Luck

2. Specialization allows workers to focus on the parts of a production process where:

    a. They work on the weekend
    b. They are at a disadvantage
    c. They feel special
    d. They have a distinct advantage

3. *True or False:* Specialization requires Trade. People in Joseph's village earned money by selling items they were good at producing, and they used the money to buy items they did not make.

    True ____
    False ____

4. Joseph's village traded with other villages, and his country traded with other countries. Select the correct portion of the Gross Domestic Product (GDP) equation below that measures trading activity between countries:

$$GDP = C + G + I + NX$$

   a. NX
   b. C
   c. I
   d. G

5. Net Exports for a country equal the value of every item exported minus the value of everything:

   a. Manufactured
   b. Imported
   c. Sold
   d. Bought on weekends

6. A generally accepted measure of a country's trading activity as a percentage of its total economic production is called the exports to GDP ratio. Correctly identify it from the equations listed below.

   a. *GDP / exports*
   b. *exports / GDP*
   c. *exports – GDP*
   d. *exports + GDP*

7. Why was Trade so necessary in Joseph's village?

    a. The people in Joseph's village were given whatever they needed by a neighboring village
    b. The people in Joseph's village earned money by employing their skills to produce what they were good at making, but they needed to buy the things they did not produce
    c. The people in Joseph's village never needed anything beyond what they produced themselves
    d. None of the answers listed are correct

Chapter 4
Supply and Demand

1. If the price of an item went up, the quantity Joseph purchased went down. If the price went down, the quantity Joseph purchased went up. His actions describe what economic theory?

   a. The theory of Relativity
   b. The law of Demand
   c. Supply theory
   d. Sunk Cost theory

2. *True or False:* The theory of Scarcity helps explain Demand theory, because people are essentially ruled by their budgets:

   True ____
   False ____

3. If the price farmers in Joseph's country received for the products they supplied was going up, they increased the quantity they supplied, and if prices were going down, they decreased the quantity supplied. What theory were they using?

   a. Demand theory
   b. The theory of Evolution
   c. The law of Supply
   d. The theory of Relativity

4. In Supply and Demand diagrams, the Demand Line always:

   a. Runs diagonally from the upper left down to the lower right
   b. Runs diagonally from the lower left up to the upper right
   c. Is a parallel line
   d. Is a vertical line

5. In Supply and Demand diagrams, the Supply Line always:

   a. Is a vertical line
   b. Runs diagonally from the upper left down to the lower right
   c. Is a parallel line
   d. Runs diagonally from the lower left up to the upper right

6. *True or False*: In Supply and Demand diagrams, the point where the Demand Line and the Supply Line cross is called the Equilibrium point, where people are willing to buy at a specific price and Suppliers are willing to sell at that price. In other words, the quantity demanded = the quantity supplied.

   True ____
   False ____

7. Regarding the direction that Supply Lines shifted in circumstances when there was increased competition or severe droughts in Joseph's country, what answer below is correct?

a. In severe droughts, they shifted to the right and with increased competition, they shifted to the left

b. In severe droughts, they shifted to the left and with increased competition, they shifted to the left

c. In severe droughts, they shifted to the right and with increased competition, they shifted to the right

d. In severe droughts, they shifted to the left and with increased competition, they shifted to the right

Chapter 5
Elasticity of Demand

1. People are more sensitive to price changes on some products than they are on others. What theory is used to explain this?

   a. Marginal utility
   b. Elasticity
   c. Opportunity costs
   d. The theory of Relativity

2. There is an equation that economists use to establish Elasticity values for products. Which equation below is correct?

   a. % change in quantity divided by % change in price
   b. % change in price divided by % change in quantity
   c. % change in quantity – % change in price
   d. % change in price + % change in quantity

3. Which statement below about Elasticity values is true:

   a. If the Elasticity value is > 1 the product is Elastic
   b. If the Elasticity value is < 1 the product is Elastic
   c. If the Elasticity value is > 1 the product is Inelastic
   d. If the Elasticity value is < 1 it is perfectly Elastic

4. Wine has an Elasticity value < 1. How sensitive was Joseph to price changes on wine?

   a. He was very sensitive to price changes
   b. He was so indifferent that he switched to lemonade
   c. His sensitivity was extremely low to price changes on wine
   d. He was so indifferent that he switched to drinking beer

5. Restaurant meals have an Elasticity value > 2. How sensitive was Joseph to price changes on restaurant meals?

   a. He was very sensitive to price changes on restaurant meals
   b. He was indifferent
   c. His sensitivity was low
   d. He didn't care, he would rather have barbecued anyway

6. A correct interpretation of Restaurant meals having an Elasticity value > 2 is:

   a. If the price for a meal goes up by 25%, the quantity demanded goes down by more than 50%
   b. If the price for a meal goes up by 25%, the quantity demanded goes down by 5%

7. A correct interpretation of a bottle of Wine having an Elasticity value of 0.5 is:

   a. If the price for a bottle of Wine goes up by 10%, the quantity demanded goes down by only 5%
   b. If the price for a bottle of Wine goes up by 10%, the quantity demanded goes down by 50%

Chapter 6
Market Structures and
Production Costs

1. There were three market structures present in Joseph's village marketplace on weekends. These were:

    a. Perfect competition, food, and spice
    b. Monopoly, perfect competition, and food
    c. Monopoly, perfect competition, and imperfect competition
    d. Perfect competition, food, and monopoly

2. Many identical items were priced the same, no matter how many merchants sold them. Economists refer to this type of market structure as:

    a. Imperfect competition
    b. Going out of business sales
    c. Monopoly
    d. Perfect competition

3. Other items were sold by several merchants in the village. These items were similar, but not the same, and the merchants priced them differently. This market structure is called:

   a. Perfect competition
   b. Imperfect competition
   c. Spice
   d. Food

4. Some items for sale were only sold by one merchant. They could not be found anywhere else in the village, and they were the highest priced items in the market-place. This kind of market structure is called:

   a. Monopoly
   b. Imperfect competition
   c. Perfect competition
   d. Food

5. In the market structure called perfect competition, the shape of the marginal revenue line is a:

   a. Vertical line
   b. Line running diagonally from upper left to lower right
   c. Line running diagonally from lower right to upper left
   d. Horizontal line

6. Joseph sold his shoes within a market structure that economists refer to as Imperfect Competition. In this market structure, similar products can be differentiated by:

   a. Physical aspects, guarantees, and perceptions
   b. Physical aspects, language, and culture
   c. Physical aspects, language, and size
   d. Size, language, and guarantees

7. Joseph sold beautiful shoes and his customers adored them, but due to the concepts of Scarcity and The Law of Demand, when new competitors entered the market, Joseph had to do what?

   a. Raise his prices and make more profits
   b. Lower his prices and break even or make less profits
   c. Keep his prices the same and go to a four-day work week
   d. None of the answers listed are correct

Chapter 7
Consumer Choices

1. If preferences alone drove decisions, people in Joseph's village would have gotten everything they wished for. An individual's income and another factor are used in consumer decisions. The other factor is:

   a. Color of the item purchased
   b. Satisfaction received from the purchase
   c. Shape of the item purchased
   d. Size of the item purchased

2. Economists refer to the satisfaction a consumer experiences when making a purchase as:

   a. Comfort
   b. Serendipity
   c. The wow factor
   d. Utility

3. *True or False*: In Utility Tables used by economists, Total Utility is shown as a cumulative value at each quantity, and it increases as quantities increase. Marginal Utility decreases as quantities increase.

True ____
False ____

4. Economists believe that Sophia would have chosen a combination of items from her Budget Constraint Model and Utility Tables that had the highest amount of:

   a. Popularity
   b. Attention from her family
   c. Total utility
   d. Compliments from her friends

5. An additional decision method Sophia may have used demonstrates that people care a lot about the level of satisfaction per dollar they spend. Using this logic, she would calculate:

   a. Marginal Utility divided by price
   b. Total Utility divided by price
   c. Marginal Utility – price
   d. Total Utility + price

6. Sophia used two methods to determine the optimal combination of Plays and Togas to purchase for her family: Total Utility and Marginal Utility per Dollar spent. It is very interesting that:

   a. Each method gave her different combinations of products
   b. Each method gave her the same combination of products
   c. Each method was used by sailors to find True North
   d. Each method was used by farmers to grow more wheat

7. Sophia's budget constraint is listed below. Knowing that Plays cost $7 and each Toga set she bought for her family cost $14, what is the correct interpretation of the points (letters) on the diagram?

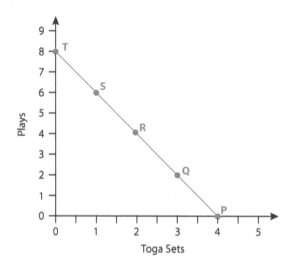

a. Each point on the diagram represents Sophia's possible purchase combinations because her monthly budget is $56

b. Each point on the diagram represents Sophia's possible purchase combinations because her monthly budget is $48

c. Each point on the diagram represents Sophia's possible purchase combinations because her monthly budget is $62

d. None of the answers listed are correct

Chapter 1
Notes

Chapter 2
Notes

Chapter 3
Notes

Chapter 4
Notes

Chapter 5
Notes

Chapter 6
Notes

Chapter 7
Notes

ABOUT THE AUTHOR

Chris Anderson has an MBA from the University of Chicago and a BA from the University of Northern Colorado. He worked in corporate banking for thirty years. In retirement, Chris has followed his passion for the  subject of Economics to become an adjunct professor of Economics at a college near his home. Along with teaching, his professional interests center on writing helpful and entertaining books.